Finding Hope When Dreams Have Shattered

By Ted Bowman

Table of Contents

Introduction

*H*ope does not easily conform to an orderly step-by-step process. A book of chapters, one building on the other does not fit well with people's experiences of hope. Hope happens! Hope is fast and slow. Hope comes and goes. Hope is personal. And we can access hope best through stories of hope.

This is a booklet of stories about hope, some heard from people along the way, others found in poetry, fiction or essay.

Hope does not easily conform to an orderly step-by-step process.

In most cases, I have added some commentary or reflection to the story or quote. Hopefully, my words will stimulate you to add your own thoughts. On a few pages, you will simply find a quote or poem or song, for your own reflection and use.

In 1994 I wrote and published a booklet about grief, a special kind of grief that I called a loss of dreams. The booklet addressed those losses that shatter images and pictures we have held of ourselves, our families, even of life itself. Loss of dreams, I suggested, could interrupt or end our future story. Plans and wishes for next year, for retirement, for health, for travel or adventure (we all have our list of plans and dreams) could get interrupted or forever changed when something unexpected and un- wanted occurred.

In the earlier booklet, I included a section on hope and healing after such losses. Almost immediately, readers asked for more about hope. What they told me was that finding hope and healing after loss was easier said than done. Even when effective grief and mourning work was done, many still found themselves focused on what was missing, on that which was lost. It was hard, some said next to impossible, to turn the corner toward hope, harder than many thought it would be. Sometimes months after their initial loss event, people still found themselves without hope, at least in propor- tion to the hope experienced before the loss.

Many focused on what was missing, on that which was lost.

Because of stories like these, I have been deliberately asking for and listening to stories of hope. "What keeps you going," I have asked. "From where does your hope come?" "How have you found hope, given what you experienced?" "What resources have you tapped for hope?" "Tell me how you have kept your hope alive." In the midst of meeting people in despair and pain, I also encountered hopeful people. As I listened to the various stories I heard amazing accounts of resiliency and strength in spite of tragedy, oppression, and loss.

What I also came to see was that people found hope in multiple ways. Something that generated or sustained hope for one person was of little use to another. Each person kept hope alive or created new hopes in their own unique and poignant ways. Hope, it seemed, is personal, idiosyncratic and individual! Even so, there was a contagious quality in being around hopeful people. In spite of their differences, people found the hope of another a catalyst for their own hope. And, so, one story often led to another ... and another ... and another. Here are some of the stories.

There was a contagious quality in being around hopeful people.

Notes About Format

t o make the booklet as readable as possible, the thoughts, words or ideas of others will be noted in the text. Credit should be given where credit is due. However, there will not be footnotes, only a full reference list at the end of the booklet.

Feel free to move about the booklet. Pick and choose sections to read. Remember hope is personal. Some of the pieces will not connect with your way of hoping. Move on. But come back later. A perspective on hope that doesn't fit for you may be a resource for a friend or family member. I also urge you to revisit sections that are useful. A second or third reading will often reveal thoughts or dimensions overlooked earlier. However you use the booklet, make it yours and use in the way that is most helpful to you.

Feel free to move
about the booklet.

The Grieving/
Hope Connections

This booklet begins with the grief/hope connection. The intimate bond between these two powerful forces — grief and hope — must be addressed. I am firmly convinced that hope and grief are part of the same stew and that one without the other, like some stews or soups, will be missing something. I'm also convinced that each is realized best when we

I am firmly convinced that hope and grief are part of the same stew.

dare to be as honest as possible about our losses, hopes and dreams. I start with a powerful statement by Anne Lamott as an example of this sort of honesty.

> *All those years I fell for the great palace lie that grief*
> *should be gotten over as quickly as possible and as*
> *privately. But what I've discovered since is that the*
> *lifelong fear of grief keeps us in a barren, isolated place*
> *and that only grieving can heal grief; the passage of time*

will lessen the acuteness, but time alone, without the direct experience of grief, will not heal it.

… The depth of the feeling (grief) continued to surprise me and threaten me, but each time it hit again and I bore it … I would discover that it hadn't washed me away. Don't get me wrong: grief sucks: it really does. Unfortunately, though, avoiding it robs us of life, of the now, of a sense of a living spirit. Mostly I have tried to avoid it by staying very busy, working too hard, trying to achieve as much as possible. You can often avoid the pain by trying to fix other people; shopping helps in a pinch, as does romantic obsession. Martyrdom can't be beat. While too much exercise works for many people, it doesn't for me, but I have found that a stack of magazines can be numbing and even mood altering. But the bad news is that whatever you use to keep the pain at bay robs you of the flecks and nuggets of gold that feeling grief will give you. A fixation can keep you nicely defined and give you an illusion that your life has not fallen apart. But since your life may indeed have fallen apart, the illusion won't hold up forever, and if you are lucky and brave, you will be willing to bear disillusion. You begin to cry and writhe and yell and then to keep on crying; and then, finally, grief ends up giving the two best things: softness and illumination (Lamott, pp. 68-73).

Lamott's candid disclosure contains the truth that grieving and hoping are inextricably intertwined. For hope to be reconstructed after significant loss requires attention to the loss that undermined hope. That can be a challenge.

After his son died, Terry Pringle described his grieving
this way.

It is six weeks before I begin grieving, before the exhilara-
tion of Eric's fight wears off, and I begin to deal with the
fact that Eric is gone. When
grief comes, it is disguised,   **Attention is required**
at first masquerading as   **to the loss that**
other forms of depression   **undermined hope.**
and anger. It jumps around
and taunts me, making me
suspect it is the leaky plumbing, the delay in repairs, an
editor slow to write, that is bothering me. Finally I
identify the emotion as grief and one day sit down to
mourn the loss of my son.

But grief is elusive, hard to grab. It visits, drains me, and
then is gone but will return. (Pringle, p. 186)

Understandably, people who have experienced loss and
these sorts of emotions will want to move on to hope
quickly, or at least to some place other than the pain of
grieving. These desires can be reinforced when after a
loss someone is told to "get on with your life" or "get
back to normal." Arthur Frank has suggested that the
problems with mourning that most people have, have
less to do with their own losses and more to do with
other people's desires that they get the mourning over
with. Accommodation, adjustment, and acceptance
become code words for moving on. In contrast, consider
this perspective.

I want to emphasize mourning as affirmation. To mourn what has passed, either through illness or death, affirms the life that has been led. To adjust too rapidly is to treat the loss as simply an incident from which one can bounce back; it devalues whom or what was lost. When an ill person loses the body in which she has lived, or when a caregiver suffers the death of the person he has cared for, the loss must be mourned fully and in its own time. Only through that mourning can we find a life on the other side of loss (Frank, p. 40).

Grieving is important, yes. But, what is grief? Clarity about terms is important. *Grief* is a whole body response to loss. That is, grieving involves our emotions, our thoughts, our bodies, our whole self. Everyone grieves. Not everyone mourns. *Mourning* is the outward expression of grieving. Some people keep their grieving to themselves. They still grieve. They just don't do it publicly, outwardly. *Bereavement* is a word used most often to describe the grief that follows death. People who have had a friend or family member die are often described as the bereaved.

Everyone grieves. But everyone does their grieving a little differently.

How do people grieve and mourn? In every way imaginable!! Some cry, others wail. Some ask questions; some want answers. Others scream or yell; many are quieter. There are those who want to be alone; many need and want friends and family close by. Some find resources like music very helpful. Some want distractions like work or just to be doing things; others find it difficult to do things in the midst of their grieving. Many talk a lot; others write their thoughts and feelings on paper.

So, you might be asking, how does one move toward hope when your life has fallen apart? The rest of this booklet and the stories contained within each chapter are an attempt to name and discuss access points for hope told to me or ones found in stories. To be sure, hope happens! It happens in a myriad of ways, some of which we can activate or construct for ourselves; others come to us. Robert Cording wrote of driving with his wife as they struggled with her father's cancer and other losses. They came upon a field of fireflies, *"And so we stopped, left the car running...Hypnotized, we followed their paths across the field, in and out of trees, their flickering drawing us farther and farther, we knew, from our purpose."* (Cording, pp. 27-28) For some hope begins with respite or with an experience that reminds them again that life has beauty in spite of the grieving.

Others perform or receive acts of kindness and support that can help restore the soul, even when doing so can be difficult. After a brutal and devastating rape, an experience that often left her alone with her grief, Patricia Weaver Francisco began to reach out slowly to others. She described beginning this way: *A skillful illusion that the pain can be shared can be a bridge to beginning again. This requires a listening infused with love and anger. A friend whose heart has many rooms can hold you up out of the water* (Francisco, p. 50). For Francisco, such a friend had to be able to listen to both grief and hope.

Mary Sheepshanks also embraced the reality that hope and grief will always be bound together. But, such ties need not block experiences of hope and change.

Four years into widowhood, my life has undergone enormous changes and I am not the same person that I was. I have become more independent and self-reliant, but also more selfish. You get out of the habit of constantly considering someone else's wishes and needs, out of the habit of ministering. If I want to turn on my light and read in the night or listen to music, then I do so. No more tiptoeing down to the kitchen to make a silent cup of tea when I can't sleep - I have a kettle by my bed. If I want to go on working in the evening I do not have to break off to get dinner. If I choose to write until midnight and then eat cold baked beans out of the tin, there is no one to see.

I still miss Charlie, sometimes with a piercing stab of longing that catches me unprepared .... (Sheepshanks, pp. 2-3).

You get out of the habit of considering someone else's wishes and needs.

This is a booklet about hope, many kinds of hope. More to the point, it is a booklet about hope in the midst of grieving. This section is crucial for what follows!

When Dreams Are Shattered — Dreaming New Dreams

hen expectations about the course of life are not met, people experience inner chaos and disruption. Such disruptions represent a loss of the future. Restoring order to life necessitates reworking understandings of the self and the world, redefining the disruption and life itself (Becker, p. 4).

My work for the last thirty years has been listening to stories of change and transition in people's lives. Along the way, people began adding something to their story. I recall that it took the form of a blurt, an exclamation, or a shout. And it appeared to be some sort of commentary or reaction to the story of disruption they were telling me. They said words like: "I never expected this to happen!" And they would often add, "to me" or "to us", or "to our family or group". Others used phrases like, "This is not fair. I played by the rules. This is not fair!" Still others posed a question or what sounded like a question. I now think it was more a statement of grief and confusion. "Why don't they warn you? Why didn't anybody tell me this could happen to us?"

For too long I didn't fully understand what the people were saying. I thought they were talking about the death, the divorce, the dismissal from work, the diagnosis just revealed, or whatever was their loss. To be sure, they were. But, I am now convinced they were also saying much more about another loss, the loss of dreams.

Loss of dreams is likened to the experience of losing an emotionally important image of oneself, one's family, one's body, one's job; losing the possibilities of "what might have been;" and abandonment of plans for a particular future. (See Bowman, 1994. Also Mitchell and Anderson, 1983).

Listen for the loss of dreams.

Here are examples. As you read, listen for loss of dreams. Even if the details of your situation are different than what you read, ask yourself if you can relate to the emotional tone being expressed? The first is a doctor's story of coming to grips with a brain injury sustained in a bicycle accident. In the midst of rehabilitation, there are these words of loss.

> … *One word, hiding in my unconscious, lying in wait on the periphery of my knowledge, had stripped me of hope and shattered my dreams.* Permanent. *My head injury was bearable only because it was temporary. Permanent injury meant I had already lost. My job. My identity. My life.*

Later the same day ...

> ...*I felt numb about my self-knowledge. I could never, at least not for very long, slip back again into my former innocence when I believed my losses were all correctable, but I still had a long way to go before reaching emotional acceptance of my head-injured persona* (Osborn, pp. 116-119).

In that poignant moment, Osborn was, I believe, beginning another rehabilitation. She was facing shattered dreams. Because of the brain injury, she was losing an emotionally important picture of herself, her work, her way of life, and her future. Those long held images and hopes also needed rehabilitative attention.

A parallel can be found in this story set on a farm, in rural America. But, it could be anywhere. Kent Meyers wrote of his and his siblings' loss of their future story after his father's death.

> *He died at a season of the year when we had no choice but to continue farming. It was April. Corn needed planting in May. There was no time to find a renter. Kevin, finishing his sophomore year of college, was certainly the most knowledgeable in what had to be done, but Mom wouldn't have him quit school. On weekends he came back from South Dakota State University and worked, but otherwise it was left to me and my two young brothers, Joel and Colin, to prepare the soil, plant the crops, and continue feeding the cattle before and after school. Land won't wait for grief. We joined together to do what we had to do* (Meyers, p. 20).

A loss of dreams can be the loss of the expected future.

The death of Ken Meyers' father rippled far beyond grieving the death of the family patriarch.

Consider also this mother coming to grips with the birth of her child.

> *When our baby was born we lost something we were already in love with - our idea of what she would be. No baby could ever completely fulfill that idea or be that fantasy, but most babies approach or overlap our dream baby, because our dreams come from what we know, for our idea of the norm. A child with a disability was not in our picture at all, except maybe as an occasional fear. We who have a child with a disability lost not only our fantasy baby, but our reliance on having a "normal" baby* (Gill, p. 16).

So, loss of dreams has to do with an important, internal picture that people carry of themselves, their family, their future, or a way of life. When shattered or taken away, some say, "I never expected this to happen!"

Everyone, wrote theologian and counselor Andrew Lester, has a core narrative or story that guides their lives.

> *I define a core narrative as the central interpretive theme that provides an individual or system with an overarching structure (composed of numerous smaller stories) that organizes and makes sense out of a particular aspect of the human condition. Our sense of self, our identity, is built piece by piece as we form our experiences into stories and then integrate these stories into our ongoing core narratives* (Lester, pp. 29-30).

After talking with hundreds of people about shattered dreams, I have become convinced that for most, loss of dreams alters their core narrative. It becomes crucial to grieve the conspicuous losses — the death, divorce, home, health, job — but

It becomes crucial to grieve the conspicuous losses and the loss of dreams.

also the loss of dreams. Ironically, coming to grips with shattered dreams is often the re-connection to hope. Many people have told me that their ability to move forward after loss has been dependent on grieving shattered dreams and creating new pictures and dreams after loss. Failure to do so has often kept someone living with old pictures or narratives still dominating their view of the world. One day a friend of mine yelled, "I don't want to be a widow." Sometime later, she told me that there was more to her than being a widow. She was beginning to create new pictures after the death of her husband. She refused to think of herself only as a couple, even half a couple. There was more to her life than that, however much she grieved her loss.

Throughout this booklet are perspectives on hope. In the face of disruptive changes, you will find stories of change and transition. In much the same way, we grieve other losses, we grieve loss of dreams. And we strive to hope again. It's not easy.

This chapter is a bit different than others in as much as the focus is shattered dreams and our understanding of them.

You will find less in this particular chapter addressing hope since that is the focus of the booklet. Too many people have faced and grieved the conspicuous loss, then struggled to find hope again. For many, it is also essential to grieve the loss of dreams. If this seems to describe your reality, I urge you to give attention to that loss as well. After grieving old dreams, new dreams can then be created.

break up.
move location

A woman had a severe case of rheumatoid arthritis. As she described its particular impact for her, she volunteered that she woke up everyday in pain. This was her conspicuous health loss. As she continued she beamed with pride about her ways of coping with the arthritis. "I've learned pain control", she said, as she described changes in diet, careful exercising, planned use of medications, even tools to help her relax. Here was a person who was coping well with a huge change. Then, her face dropped, tears flowed, as she said, "Ted, inside I am still a dancer and that is so very hard to let go of."

"Inside I am still a dancer."

This was her loss of dreams. Dancing for her was exercise, body image, her social outlet, even a significant part of her way of life. And no one had helped her grieve or adjust to this loss.

I asked if she had grieved her shattered dreams. She was taken aback. She knew about funerals, retirement events, not grieving for dancing. I suggested that she go to the dance hall at least one more time with her friends. Use the occasion, I suggested, to tell each other stories about the dancing and its meaning for each. Honor the richness of that part of her life by a rite of passage to mark the change. It would also be, I submitted, a time for grieving.

Then, after some grieving, it seemed that she

We all tell stories of things we no longer do ... but keep alive through our stories.

had at least three options. One, to put the dancing on the imaginary shelf, never to be done again, but kept alive as a rich part of her story telling life. (We all tell stories of things we no longer do but which we keep alive through our stories.) A second option was to continue dancing using her canes, wheel chair or other mobility aids. It was important to note that consideration of this option involved grieving because the dancing to be done this way would be different than the way she wanted to dance. Still a third choice was for her to become a coach or teacher of others who wanted to dance, thereby keeping the dancing alive.

Dreaming new dreams and creating new pictures, after disruptive change and loss, involves grieving old dreams.

Have you experienced a loss of dreams? What is your loss? Naming it is a necessary task in the move toward grieving and hoping.

In the Aftermath of Tragedy: Realistic Hope

On September 11, 2001 the unthinkable happened. All the assumptions about terrorism, war, even conceived acts of community violence, were shattered as highjacked planes were flown into the Pentagon in Washington, DC and the World Trade Center in New York City. In response, many people wrote or said that the world would never be the same again.

The world would never be the same again.

This booklet was being finished when those events occurred.

Hope is especially challenged when there is a kind of loss that affects a whole community, nation or world. A few years ago I was invited to a small rural town in Minnesota that had experienced too many deaths in a short period for a town that size. Even though each person who died was honored in their own way by their family and friends, the town leaders knew that the town itself had been affected. A community day of grief and mourning was arranged. It was a wise and caring act.

Similar actions have been taken in response to tornadoes, hurricanes, floods, forest fires, shootings and other destructive events. There was a massive show of support for the citizens of Oklahoma City after the bombing of the Federal Building in 1995. In all these examples, individuals, their families and a larger community were affected. This contrasts with most losses that while often large and significant for those directly connected, the larger community is less aware or even unaware that a personal grief has transpired.

The events of September 11 were magnified versions, and more, of those earlier community tragedies. In this brief section, the question to be addressed is what, then, can be said about grief and hope in the face of such events? Here is a suggested list of perspectives and actions steps that can address the grief, facilitate mourning and promote hope in the aftermath of tragedy.

✒ *Stable and continuing support is crucial when our worlds are turned upside down.*

When the ground gets shaky (one person called it a crack in my universe), it is important to have a supportive hand to hold. If the neighborhood (our immediate world) seems unsafe, one of the most important elements of security is stable and continuing support. In New York, after the attacks on the World Trade Center, strangers supported each other in ways that didn't

25

conform to the stereotype of a bustling metropolitan area. That was wonderful and powerful. Support that transcends social barriers is especially significant. Equally important is the ongoing support for people whose lives continue to bear loss or trauma. Crisis intervention at the time of an incident is crucial. Support two and three months later, and later after that, is also needed. Sections of this booklet further address the importance of support after loss.

✒ Empathy and outreach to those directly affected helps them and those giving support.

One of the reactions after a community tragedy is what can be called identification. "That could have been me," some say. Survivors identify with those directly affected or those who died while they are still living. Empathy, of this kind, can be a resource as long as the guilt is not overdone. In the aftermath of September 11, I tried, through writing, to identify with those affected AND to note how I was different. Here are some lines from a poem I wrote:

My feelings heightened AND numbed
Just as they experienced emotions no one should ever face

My lungs gasped, easy breathing interrupted
Their lungs filled with fire and dust

My stomach turned
Too many had eaten their last meal

My tear ducts opened
About the time their air ducts collapsed

...My life was turned upside down
A building imploded on theirs

I observed
They experienced

I wanted to do something/anything
Their choices were limited

I had distance
They were too, too close for comfort

These distinctions are crucial
Still we were joined and always will be
Death of this kind is contagious
I now live with it   (Bowman, 2001)

✒ Community events, public rites, rituals and other visible responses can be helpful.

As noted above, it is important when there is a community tragedy that the community gathers in some fashion to acknowledge and respond to the tragedy. It is the collective version of what happens when an individual dies. When that occurs, the person's community or inner circle gathers around. At their best, these rituals provide some meaning and stability during a time of ambiguity and confusion. (See Pauline Boss's book, *Ambiguous Loss*.)

✒ Be aware that "local and personal" losses will be affected by national or community events.

Within twenty-four hours of the planes crashing into the World Trade Centers, my aging father was taken to the hospital because of chest pains. Even though quickly reassured that he was in no danger, there was something about the proximity of the national loss and the scare about my father's health and life that made the news of his hospitalization harder to hear. It was as if I was on overload. It was too much at one time. Be aware that our losses accumulate and that we often are dealing with more than one at a time. Be kind to yourself or to others if there are personal losses to face in the midst of a community tragedy.

🖋 *Try to separate your grieving from your political or personal response to those culpable or the ways the events are handled.*

Anger at the drunken driver, the shooter that randomly included someone you care about, or at terrorists, is understandable. Indignation deserves its place as we respond to tragedies. Many who have become effective advocates for change or response started with anger and hurt. Remember to also give attention to the grief and loss. Sorrow and anger can be connected. But each deserves time and attention.

🖋 *Hope can be rekindled or restored by focussing on hopeful actions.*

- By acts of care for self and others
- By future commitments, even in the next few hours
- By writing, music, talking ... to make sense of and to give voice to your thoughts and feelings
- By connections to life in the midst of death.

(When asked how to respond to children after September 11, many child development specialists suggested that as much or more attention be given to the acts of heroism performed by rescue workers than on a recitation of the many who died. Note it was not an either/or, but rather a both/and.)

- By practice of disciplines like the serenity prayer - awareness of what you can change, what you can not, and the wisdom to know the difference.
- By telling and hearing stories of hope such as this one passed to me in the days following September 11.

A Native American grandfather was talking to his grandson about how he felt about the tragedy on September 11th.

He said, "I feel as if I have two wolves fighting in my heart. One wolf is the vengeful, angry, violent one. The other wolf is the loving, compassionate one."

The grandson asked him, "Which wolf will win the fight in your heart?"

The grandfather answered, "The one I feed."

Feed your hope.

A Page for Your Reflections

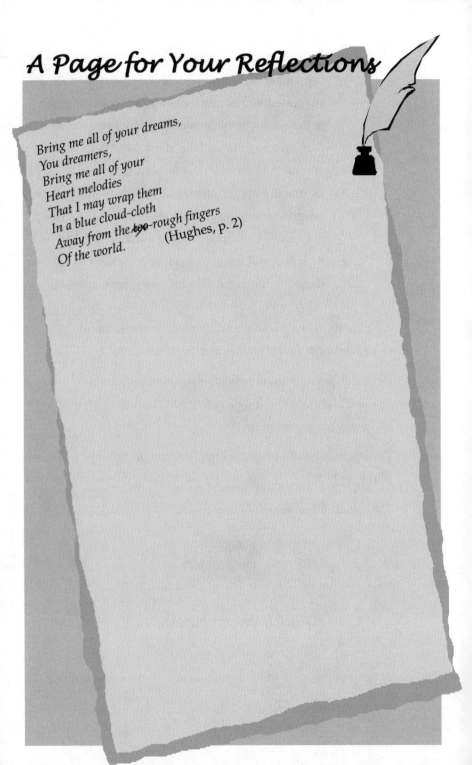

Bring me all of your dreams,
You dreamers,
Bring me all of your
Heart melodies
That I may wrap them
In a blue cloud-cloth
Away from the ~~too~~-rough fingers
Of the world.   (Hughes, p. 2)

Many Kinds of Hope

*H*ope is important, but we have been too limited in the
kind of hope we prescribe...Our idea that the only
kind of hope is hope for cure limits what we can offer.
There are, in fact, many kinds of hope: hope for a good
period of life ahead, hope for enriching relationships, hope
for control of pain, hope for a strong sense of care and
support from your doctors (Spiegel, p. 104).

Hope is limited only by our creativity and our courage.
Locking onto one particular hope shuts the door on
many other possibilities, AND, in so doing, we may
reduce or eliminate some of the energy, support, accomplishment or satisfaction we
need to keep going. We
may create our own barriers
to what we need most to
keep hope alive.

*Locking onto one
particular hope shuts
the door on many
other possibilities*

Many who have only one hope, let's call it the hope for cure, often say that they are hoping against hope. I don't think they mean against, if against means opposite. I think they mean hope onto hope. They are putting all their hope eggs in the one basket. Such hope is common. We all do it! In the face of tremendous odds or contrary evidence, we still hope for cure, we hope for more time, we hope that our job will not be the one eliminated, we hope that our mate will stop drinking, or we hope to live until a certain date.

Many people find this kind of hope essential to keep going. It serves as a motivator, a catalyst. Others will adjust their hopes more in keeping with all the information they possess. Remember people vary widely in the ways they cope with adversity in their lives. We can't impose our preferred ways of handling a tough situation onto someone else. Furthermore, our ability to be strong in response to one situation does not mean that we will be as strong for the next challenge.

What do you hope for today?

Regardless of which way you pursue hope, I encourage you to find other hopes as well. What do you hope for today? Are there things you want to say to someone you care about before it's too late … no matter how long you have to live? Is there something you have been putting off doing ("I hope to get to that sometime") and now is the time to get started? Even if there is little time left, what do you wish to say or do?

The quote from David Spiegel (page 34), a physician and cancer researcher, reflects his experience with women facing a terminal diagnosis related to their breast cancer. He discovered a kind of resiliency and strength in those women who dared to hope in spite of their prognosis. Further, their strength was connected to a willingness to hope for more than cure. Such hopes could be small and large, private and social, internal and environmental, or immediate and far away.

Audre Lorde expressed similar wisdom well before Spiegel's studies:

> ...I'd give anything not to have cancer and my beautiful breast gone, fled with my love of it. But then immediately after I guess I have to qualify that - there really are some things I wouldn't give.

Then, she wrote eloquently about her poetry, her friends, her children, even her senses. Finally, she reflected on her priorities with these words.

> So I guess I do have to be careful that my urgencies reflect my priorities (Lorde, p. 76).

I believe that such an attitude could benefit all of us.

One writer put it that hope is the thing that gets people out of bed in

Call hope a wake-up call.

the morning. If that is the case, and I believe it can be, wouldn't it be wiser for us to have several things to hope for each day? Call it safety in numbers. Call it ambitious. Call it seeing hope as a resource, not just a rescue. Call hope a wake-up call. Call it what you will. Hope can take many forms. Therefore, hope for many things!

Teaching Ourselves Joy Again

F inding joy after loss can seem like a contradiction, a nice thought, but next to impossible to achieve. Grieving people often speak of a preoccupation with what was lost. It seems, they tell me, that they grieve the loss only to grieve it again ... and again. It becomes hard, at times, to start over, to turn the corner to life after loss.

As you will find on other pages of this booklet, it IS crucial to do the grieving, however hard and difficult it may be. Too many of us try to hurry, avoid, or move quickly beyond our grief.

Too many of us try to hurry, avoid, or move quickly beyond our grief.

But, I am presuming that you have begun to face your loss. You have at least started the journey of grief that C. S. Lewis described as a long and winding valley. And you yearn for some light, some joy, at the end of the valley.

What, you might be asking, is the connection between joy and hope? Hope, as these pages suggest, takes many forms and contain many elements. Among them is an attitude of peaceful joy. Consider this distinction from Susanna Tamaro.

> *The loss of joy, I must say, is the thing I have mourned more than any other. Later, indeed, I felt happiness, but happiness is to joy as an electric light-bulb is to the sun. Happiness is always caused by something; you are happy about something, it is a feeling that comes from the outside. Joy, on the other hand, is not caused by anything. It possesses you for no apparent reason; it is essentially rather like the sun, which gives off heat thanks to the combustion of its own core* (Tamaro, p. 55).

Noted novelist and essayist, Barbara Kingsolver, offered some personal insights that may in a first reading sound more like happiness than joy. Read again with more care:

> *In my own worst seasons I've come back from the colorless world of despair by forcing myself to look hard, for a long time, at a single glorious thing: a flame of red geranium outside my bedroom window. And then another: my daughter in a yellow dress. And another: the perfect outline of a full, dark sphere behind the crescent moon. Until I learned to be in love with my life again. Like a stroke victim retraining new parts of the brain to grasp lost skills, I have taught myself joy, over and over again* (Kingsolver, p. 15).

A single glorious thing. A geranium. A child. The moon. Nancy Mairs writing about her life with multiple sclerosis declared that she would not want to wish MS on anyone. But, as part of her adjustment, she was forced to become more aware of details, little things that could throw her off balance, cause her to fall. In so doing, she also became aware of other details she would not have seen had she not had MS, things like geraniums, small animals, and nuances of color (Mairs, pp. 114-115). Joy comes in the strangest ways. And sometimes we have to teach ourselves how to be joyful again. And it may start with, as Tamaro wrote, something from the outside, what she called happiness. Happiness can lead to joy when the happiness somehow connects with the joyful centering part of who I am. And when joyful, I am also hopeful.

Sometimes we have to teach ourselves how to be joyful again.

I'm reminded of an older friend who when hospitalized in great pain was given a Walkman so that she could hear the music she loved. Her hospital experience became all the less oppressive and scary.

Another woman told me that she had associated happiness so firmly with marriage that when hers ended, she did not allow herself to fully experience joy and delight. Seven years later, when I met her, she used the metaphor of shooting herself in the foot. "Yes," she said, "I *would like to find a man, a partner to share life. But, I'm now ready to see that I can be happy whether I find a man or not.*" She had come to realize that she had deprived herself of joy and delight because of believing that happiness could only be found in marriage. She still wished to be married. Now, in contrast to that earlier period, she saw that happiness and joy could be found in multiple places and in varied ways. She also now believed that in spite of being deprived of something she fervently wanted, she could still find joy.

What small things bring you happiness or joy?

What small things bring you happiness or joy? Name some sounds, sights, tastes, or touches you would enjoy ... now. Choose some that are possible even in your condition. Don't dwell for the moment on those senses you can't enjoy. Find your single glorious thing. Find a gift you can give someone who is grieving. Create joy!

sunlight
& green trees
bumble bees
& kitties
purring —
humor &
laughter
praying

Create joy!

Supportive Care

*I*t's one thing to face adversity by your self; it's quite another when you have someone in your corner. There is something amazingly powerful in supportive friends, family, words, deeds, and what many people describe as "presence." Support, you see, is not only given and received. There is also the phenomenon of "perceived support." Again and again in response to questions about hope, the most common responses were related to supportive family and friends.

What kept you going?

Ram Dass and Paul Gorman wrote of a person who had experienced a stroke and the resulting rehabilitation, who, in spite of quality care at many levels, could say:

I have never, ever, met someone who sees me as whole .... Can you understand this? Can you? No one sees me and helps me to see myself as being complete, as is. Everything else is Band-Aids, you know (Dass and Gorman, p. 27).

Christina Middlebrook challenged her daughter who was having a really tough time talking to and about her mother's cancer:

> *Talking about my dying is not going to kill me. Not talking about it will not save my life* (Middlebrook, p. 31).

When facing stroke, death or some other loss, we yearn for support. It is essential for healing, recovery, and life itself. We want companions as we walk that lonesome valley. Those who have studied support tell us that it can come in many forms. We often think of emotional support first and foremost. And, yes, emotional support is important, if not crucial, for many. But, there are many other forms of support,

We want companions as we walk that lonesome valley.

My wife and I were leaving the nursing home with a friend whose husband's health was slowly, but steadily deteriorating. *"How else can we be helpful?"* we inquired. She looked back suspiciously; *"Do you really mean what you are asking?"* (Support, she was reminding us, is frequently offered in words but not in deeds which match the words.) *"Yes,"* we affirmed. Then, with a voice of hesitancy, she asked, *"Would you be willing to clean the house? I hate to go home every night to a dirty house and I have no energy to do an adequate cleaning."* She wanted tangible support, hands-on support. It is a significant form of support, especially when accompanied by emotional caring.

Would you be willing to clean the house?

Still another form is what some call esteem support. Grief has a way of diminishing confidence, ability and hope. Restoration of esteem can be encouraged from within ourselves and from others. Individually, we can reach into our memory banks and recall times and situations that would have taxed anyone and somehow, someway, we found the courage and resources to meet and address the challenge. With our friends and family,

We can be that memory person.

we can be that memory person, reminding someone of resourcefulness they may not see at the moment but which they exhibited at some earlier time. Further, our belief that they can handle the situation may be sufficient to inspire them when they have little faith in their own abilities.

So, support can take many forms. We must be careful, however not to take it for granted. Many people experience their most severe pain at the absence of support from those they thought would be there for them. After a cancer diagnosis, Arthur Frank wrote for many when

We must be careful not to take support for granted.

he said that he and his wife expected that when the worst happened, friends and family would respond with care and involvement. Then the worst happened and they no longer expected, they knew. *Some came through and others disappeared.* (Frank, p. 38)

as always you find out who your friends are —

*H*ere is a list of suggestions that can help to make support real. They are offered both for those grieving and for those offering support.

- Take initiative. The grieving should not be the ones to initiate their own care.

- If you're the griever, not the caregiver, take initiative anyway. Even though grievers should be the recipients of care, don't let its absence continue. "I'm having a tough week. Could you spare an hour or so one evening?" Letting your friends know some time limits can help them in providing the care you need.

- Be creative! A friend bought supportive cards for herself. As wonderful as my friends are, she told me, you don't always get a card when you need one. I wanted some around the house just in case.

- Let the griever lead! I often ask grieving friends, "Do you want to talk about "up" things or "down" things ... or not talk at all?" Let the griever guide.

- A friend, mother of a child with Rett Syndrome, convened a required meeting of family and friends. Their worst fears were that she would ask for care of the child, whose condition scared them and their ability to handle the situation. Rather, she had lists of other support needs — mowing, shopping, a massage, household repairs, driving — things that if done could free her for greater quality care for her daughter.

🍃 Remember there are many forms of support. If words are not your strength, then ask about driving, cleaning, repairing .... "How can I be helpful to you now?" Many people report that they don't know what to say. When and if that is the case, then do something, even sit with someone. Words are not always the best form of support.

🍃 Hope also involves a willingness to receive support. Some cut off the very support they need by their unwillingness to allow friends and family to give support. To be sure, the sort of support offered may not be what is needed or wanted. If so, a conversation between caregivers and care-receivers can be crucial.

How do you best receive support?

How do you best receive support?

thankfully, altho this is not my natural tendency

The Peace of Wild Things

One of the commonly sought places for healing is the natural world. For many there is something about just being "outside" that promotes hope and recovery. For others, walking, rolling, or moving, while surrounded by natural beauty and growth, provides peace and healing. Some even bring a bit of the "outside" inside thereby creating a nurturing environment of plants, smells, and other natural things they love so much. When I ask people to describe what it is about the natural world that generates hope or healing, I get many responses.

For some, to be surrounded by life — birds, trees, animals, flowers, moss, moving water — helps to restore their life, even for some in the face of dying.

There is something about the mystery of the seasons

For others, there is something about the mystery of the seasons and the way that, even in places like Minnesota where I live, spring does indeed come after the long, cold winter and breeding hope within them.

For many, their most intimate and firm experience of God is found in nature. People often tell me of spiritual homes they have found by a lakeside, halfway up a hill, sitting under a tree or in a garden. When faith in self or humankind falters, there is something restorative about a natural world of ecological balance and beauty.

Still others tell me of feeling more grounded when near the actual ground. When life gets shaky for them, they head to the countryside.

The natural world can be a valuable resource for hope.

However it happens, the natural world can be a valuable resource for hope. A woman woke up one day quite depressed about her losses. She called a friend and asked for help with child-care. The woman knew she was not going to be a good parent that particular day. She wanted to avoid inflicting her depression on her children. Fortunately, her friend was able to take the children for the day and while gathering them and their gear, she told the woman that she wanted her to find at least a few minutes sometime during the day to spend in the sunshine. The woman did. Doing that among other things helped lift her spirits.

Wendell Berry, essayist, poet, and storyteller, describes the value of nature for him in this powerful poem:

When despair for the world grows in me
and I wake in the night at the least sound
in fear of what my life and my children's lives may ⸱
I go and lie down where the wood drake
rests in his beauty on the water, and the great heron feeds.
I come into the peace of wild things
who do not tax their lives with forethought
of grief. I come into the presence of still water.
And I feel above me the day-blind stars —the day stars
waiting for their life. For a time
I rest in the grace of the world, and am free.   (Berry, p. 69)

I come into the peace of wild things.

Find your own haven or rest and refreshment and lie in
the peace that comes with wild things. Give yourself
this gift!

The Paradox of Perspective

*O*ne of the most common ways for promoting hope is comparison. There is always someone worse off, we are often told, someone whose plight is more tragic or painful. Someone once called this downward comparison. Comparative pain, it seems, is supposed to cheer us up, make things better.

Another word to describe the intention of comparison is perspective. It is believed, evidently, that if the widow, the newly divorced, or the one fired or dismissed from a job could see their plight with perspective, then they would not over-react. "Look at what you do have." "You can always find something or someone else." "Look on the bright side." Think of the many phrases or words we use to encourage perspective, whether by downward or upward comparison.

Think of the many phrases or words we use to encourage.

It was in response to such attempts at helping me that I
wrote the following poem:

Too Many Platitudes

I went looking for hope the other day
Looking, it appears, in the wrong places.
Instead of acknowledgement of my grief
I got cheerfulness and
> *optimism*
> *distance*
> *easy faith   and*
> *platitudes.*

Many platitudes, too many platitudes,
Which instead of comfort raised questions,
Hard questions,
For which I have few if any answers.

Tell me, will you, how do **THE** *tough get going?*
For, you see, my tough did the going, not me.

If all you can say is something good, the rule of many,
There are days and weeks when I will be speechless.
Tell me, tell me how is that helpful?

I was told to look on the bright side, look for the silver lining.
Don't they know it's hard to see bright in the dark?

Don't feel bad, you can get a new one, someone suggested.
New, I wanted to scream, is not always better and I'm not
> *ready for new right now!*

Someone reminded me that God does not give more than
you can take.
Tell that to Jesus, I thought.
Remember "My God, why have you forsaken me?"
I'm with Jesus on that one.

I was told to keep my chin up
Tell me how, when my grief,
like a heavy magnet, is pulling in the opposite direction?

Look at what you do have, some said.
Try that, I say,

Be wary of platitudes.

Be wary, my friends, of platitudes. When someone is
looking for hope, they need more than cheerful but empty
words. At least I did. I need you more than your words.

(Bowman, 1998)

In my experience, platitudes of comparison and
perspective are of little help, especially in the early days
of grieving. Grieving people tell me that what they want
is validation, empathy, space to grieve, support for
crying or screaming ... not a forced cheer-up through
comparison or perspective. Further, I'm told — it is
also my experience — that when in the throes of mourning,
it is very difficult to see beyond yourself and gain
perspective by viewing others. There were moments
when I didn't think I would ever get better or over
a loss I had experienced.

When asked by a friend when she would once again be her old self, Ruth Coughlin, whose husband had recently died, responded.

*Maybe someday I'll be a version of the person I once was ....
but I think I have to tell you that it is impossible to watch
your husband die for ten months and then think that you
will ever be the same again.* (Couglin, pp. 34-35)

The paradox is that we need perspective. It is important to avoid over or under-reacting to our loss. The issue, I think, is not the offer of perspective. Rather, it is the timing. When someone is fully aware of their loss and grieving, perspective of the "cheer-up" type I've described is rarely helpful. However, when you are willing to be with me at my worst moments, my deepest experiences of sorrow, then I will likely be much more open to the perspective you can offer at a later time. Hope includes more than anticipation of a better future.

Are you willing to be with me at my worst moments?

Hope, at its best, can be offered and received in the worst of moments.

So, help me find perspective. But, be careful about the timing of your perspective!

A Page for Your Reflections

Let the Children Teach Us

Sometimes the best help comes from children. Sometimes hope is activated and renewed by being around children. Sometimes children teach us.

Two examples:

"Granny," he said. "Do you ever want to talk about Grandpa, or do you never want to talk about him?"

"Well," I said cautiously, knowing this might be important, and anxious not to get it wrong. "There are times when I need to talk about him very much, when it helps me. But I suppose there are other times when I feel I can't, either because it hurts too much, or because it feels private at that particular moment. On the whole, I want to talk."

He sat and digested this in silence, then he gave me a brilliant smile.

> ## There are times when I need to talk [and] other times when I feel I can't.

"I see," he said. "I see. So it's really all right to do what you feel like?"

This little boy voiced so clearly what often remains a problem for much older people.

"Yes," I said.

"Let's talk about him then," he said. So we did.

I think it is interesting that this little boy voiced so clearly what often remains a problem for much older people. So often people find it hard to broach the subject of death to the bereaved. Perhaps our airing of the subject that day will stand this child in good stead later in life, and help him to feel at ease with making approaches to friends who have suffered a loss.

During the rest of that summer, he would often bring up the subject of his grandfather when he came to stay. "It's a nice feeling," he said one day when the children were helping me water pot plants in the greenhouse, "to think we're looking after Grandpa's flowers for him." (Sheepshanks, pp. 140-141)

A few years ago the second of two cat brothers, both long-time and loved members of our household, was dying. Our almost three-year old grandson stayed with us one day a week at that time. So, he was aware of and included in some of the care as Rumple got weaker. A few days after Rumple had died, I was working in the basement and decided to throw away some well-worn towels and blanket shreds the cat had used for a quiet place in a cooler part of the house. As I carried the items to the garbage cans for pick-up the next day, my grandson saw me and yelled frantically to my wife, "What's he doing with Rumple's things?" Immediately, she began to cry. The loss was hard for her.

I returned to the house, not knowing any of this had transpired, and faced my tearful wife and an agitated three year old. I also faced a wise and caring three year old. My grandson turned to me and exclaimed, "Grammy's sad!" To which I responded, scrambling to catch up with what was going on, "What do you think we should do?" He said, "Tell her a story."

So, I sat on the floor near him and began, "Once upon a time there was an old guy and a boy who went for a walk ...." I stopped, hoping this could be a sequential tale. He immediately picked up and off he and I went for several back and forth additions about an old man and a boy. He, then, interrupted me and pointed, "Look, Grammy's smiling." "What do you think happened?" I asked. To which he instantly responded, "Grampy, stories work!"

Grampy, stories work!

These are two stories involving children. In one case a child aids a grieving widow by his honesty and obvious love for her and for his grandfather. In the second, the death is not directly addressed. Yet, healing and hope were aided by a child's resourcefulness.

Hope sometimes comes from unexpected sources, including children. Perhaps a child can be a resource of hope for you.

Narrative Surrender: NO! NEVER!

This booklet is primarily about forms of hope and ways they can be activated. It is also important that we be aware of anything that can undermine hope. *Hopelessness* can find reinforcement if and when our stories are not heard, when our stories are not validated, or when our stories are superseded by stories that "someone" deems more important. Laguna story teller and fiction writer, Leslie Silko, wrote that you don't have anything if you don't have the stories (Silko, p. 2). Someone once told me that Malcolm X said that a people without a story are like a tree without roots. Each of these writers, in response to a majority culture that too often imposed its story on those different, knew something powerful about stories.

> *People without a story are like a tree without roots.*

Anatole Broyard, in his memoir of illness, wrote about physicians:

> *"To the typical physician my illness is a routine incident in his rounds, while for me it's the crisis of my life. I would feel better if I had a doctor who was aware of this incongruity* (Broyard, p. 43).

He did not want his story to be surrendered to the medical team. Similarly, Arthur Frank chose the words used in the title of this section.

> *The story of illness that trumps all others in the modern period is the medical narrative. The story told by the physician becomes the one against which all others are ultimately judged true or false, useful or not .... I under-stand this obligation of seeking medical care as a narrative surrender .... The ill person not only agrees to follow medical regimens that are prescribed; she also agrees, tacitly but with no less implication, to tell her story in medical terms.* (Frank, pp. 5-6)

Let me be clear. The choice of these two readings is not a polemic about physician behavior. I have heard similar comments about bereavement workers, counselors, even friends and family members.

If our stories are not heard or valued, hope can be undermined.

The point being made is that our stories are significant AND that if and when our stories are not heard or valued, hope can be undermined.

What is your story? And has is it been truly heard? The late Shel Silverstein wrote about validation this way:

Said the little boy, "Sometimes I drop my spoon."
Said the old man, "I do that too."

The little boy whispered, "I wet my pants."
"I do that too," laughed the old man.
Said the little boy, "I often cry."
The old man nodded, "So do I."
"But worst of all," said the boy, " it seems
Grown-ups don't pay attention to me."
And he felt the warmth of a wrinkled old hand.
"I know what you mean," said the old man.

I do that too.

(Silverstein, p. 105)

Intergenerational validation. Each let the other know that their story was being heard.

What is hope? How is it generated? What keeps hope alive? In this booklet many responses are suggested. But, an essential element of hope is the belief and conviction that one's story will be heard. Even if it is a story one does not want to tell. "I don't want to be a widow." "No, not me, it can't be cancer." When someone is dealing with grief, especially losses that alter one's identity or self-perception, the story becomes all the more important.

Telling people, does not come easy, and neither does
listening. Seriously ill people are wounded not just in
body but in voice. They need to become storytellers in order
to recover the voices that illness and its treatment often take
away. The voice speaks the mind and expresses the spirit...
(Frank, p. xii.).

56

Have your told your story? If not, with whom might it
be shared? Writing the story, telling the story to another,
finding your story in someone else's account ... these are
all ways our stories find voice. As challenging as it can
be to break the silence or a family rule about certain
conversations, it is
crucial that our *Have your told your story?*
stories be told.
However, be
discreet. Don't unnecessarily add to your distress by
impulsively telling your story to someone that cannot
offer the support you need. Choose carefully. Sometimes friends can hear things that family members can
not, in part because family members are grieving also.
The important action is to find a way to voice your story.

Surround Yourself With Hopeful People

Almost without exception those who survived a tragedy gave credit to one person who stood by them, supported them, and gave them a sense of hope (see Bob Veninga's book, *The Gift of Hope*, an excellent resource).

Think about it. We assume that the person without hope should be the one to find or create hope. Here is an all too common example: a woman who had just recently become a widow was asked by one of her best friends when she would return to her normal self. Her response was that she would never do so. Return to normal, no. Her normal was a new normal! No one could spend weeks, she was convinced, watching his or her husband die, only to return miraculously to normal. She knew all too well that any normality in her life would now include his dying and death.

A new normal.

This new widow was not hopeless, but she did yearn for more loving care from her friends.

There are moments when our hope well is either drying out or empty and the only source of water available is hopeful people. Indeed, an act of self-care in the midst of loss can be to surround yourself with hopeful people. In my experience, hope is contagious! Not always immediately or to the same degree as those around me, but still contagious. The hope of

Hope is contagious!

others buffers my despair. It serves as an antidote to my depression. The hope of others informs me that there may be an alternative to the way I feel. And the firm belief of others that I will make it (their hope) can begin to convince me of just that.

Cornel West moved the discussion of support beyond an individual and family focus with his insights about race and culture. In *Race Matters*, he wrote:

> *The major enemy of black survival in America has been and is neither oppression nor exploitation but rather the nihilistic threat — that is, loss of hope and absence of meaning. For as long as hope remains and meaning is preserved, the possibility of overcoming oppression stays alive.*
>
> *The genius of our black foremothers and forefathers was to create powerful buffers to ward off the nihilistic threat. These buffers consisted of cultural structures of meaning*

... primarily of black religious and civic
institutions that sustained familial and communal
networks of support (West, p. 15).

Take note of his emphasis on the power of individual
AND organizational hope.

At a more personal level, Kay Redfield Jamison has
written eloquently about her life struggle with manic-
depressive illness. Even though writing about the care
she received from her psychiatrist, she could have been
writing about friends. These are her descriptive words:

> *The debt I owe my psychiatrist is beyond description ....*
> *all the compassion and warmth I felt from him that could*
> *not have been said; all the intelligence, competence, and*
> *time he put into it; and his granite belief that mine was a*
> *life worth living* (Jamison, p. 118).

She surrounded herself with hopeful people. All of us,
when facing racial prejudice, mental illness, or other
challenges need to activate resources of hope. Hopeful
people can aid us at the individual or collective level in
filling our own reservoirs of hope. Here is a specific way
this has been attempted with persons facing a cancer
procedure. Rachel Naomi Remen described the process
in her book, *Kitchen Table Wisdom.*

> *I suggest [that the person with cancer] meet together with*
> *some of their closest friends and family the day before*
> *their procedure. It does not matter how large or small the*

group is, but it is important that it be made up of those
who are connected to (the person) through a bond of
the heart.

Before this meeting I suggest [that the person] find an
ordinary stone, a piece of the earth, big enough to fit into
the palm of their hand and bring it to the meeting with
them. The ritual begins by having everyone sit in a circle.
In any order they wish to speak, each person tells the
story of a time when they, too, faced a crisis. People may
talk about the death of important persons, the loss of jobs
or of relationships, or even about their own illnesses. The
person who is speaking holds the stone the patient has
brought. When they finish telling their story of survival,
they take a moment to reflect on the personal quality that
they feel helped them
through that difficult time.
People will say such things
as, "What brought me
through was determination,"
"What brought me through was faith," "What brought
me through was humor." When they have named the
quality of their strength, they speak directly to the person
preparing for surgery or treatment, saying, "I put
determination in this stone for you," or, "I put faith into
this stone for you."

What brought me through was faith.

... After everyone has spoken the stone is given back to the
patient, who takes it with them to the hospital, to keep
nearby and hold in their hand when things get hard
(Remen, p. 152).

What a lovely ritual of passing learnings, resiliency and hope from those who have experienced a rough time in their lives to a friend, colleague or family member now facing a challenging situation.

I urge you to create a support group of hopeful people. As you do, ponder these words from Norman Cousins, modified to include hopeful friends.

Reassurance is a way of putting the human spirit to work.

Reassurance is not a Pollyanna concoction aimed at deception .... It is a way of putting the human spirit to work; a way of summoning all one's strength and resources .... No one would argue against the logic and necessity for a patient to reach out for the best medical help available. Why, then, argue against reaching within oneself — or in one's circle of friends *— for the best that the human apothecary has to offer? Reassurance and hope are ways of activating that apothecary* (Cousins, pp. 65-66).

A Page for Your Reflections

My life is a lesson in losses .... Thanks to multiple sclerosis, one thing after another has been wrenched from my life — dancing, driving, walking, working — and I have learned neither to yearn after them nor to dread further deprivation but to attend to what I have (Mairs, pp. 1014).

Alive Living: Words of Inspiration

As you have discovered in this booklet, key resources for my own coping have been and are the stories of resilient people whether told to me directly, through a second-hand source, or read in literature. I have found particular inspiration when I have read or heard a perspective — no, more an attitude — about life and living that moves my heart and head toward awe and the desire to emulate their behavior or attitude. Here are four examples. Each lifts my spirit and fosters hope because the writers chose nobleness

Writers chose nobleness and grace.

and grace in the face of circumstances that could have led to defeat and depression.

The first is Nazim Hikmet, a Turkish poet, who was a political prisoner for 18 years and who also spent the last 13 years of his life in exile.

In his powerful poem, "On Living," there are these lines:

Living is no laughing matter;
you must live with great seriousness
like a squirrel, for example —
I mean without looking for something beyond
and above living,
I mean living must be your whole occupation.

Then, the inspiring
words of hope and
courage, *"We'll still live*
with the outside, With its
people and animals, struggle and wind … for the world must
be loved this much if you're going to say 'I lived'" (Hikmet,
pp. 128-130).

Living must be your whole occupation.

Like Viktor Frankl, who in the concentration camps
chose to look for life rather than death, thereby holding
onto his world of meaning, Hikmet chose life.

A similar affirmation can be found in the words of the
American poet Mary Oliver. In a powerful counterpoint to
those who avoid talking about death, Oliver affirmed life
even as she wrote directly and poignantly about death.

When death comes
like the hungry bear in autumn;
when death comes and takes all the bright coins
from his purse

to buy me, and snaps the purse shut;
when death comes
like the measle-pox;

when death comes
like an iceberg between the shoulder blades

What powerful metaphors and images, Oliver created to aid the reader in facing the reality of death. There is no flinching or hesitancy. She named the reality of death as she saw it. And then, she demonstrated a rare congruence in the way of living and dying. When death comes, she wrote,

> *I want to step through the door full of curiosity,*
> > *wondering:*
> *what is it going to be like, that cottage of darkness?*

The poem ends with these inspiring words of hope and courage:

> *When it's over, I don't want to wonder*
> *if I have made of my life something particular, and real.*
> *I don't want to find myself sighing and frightened,*
> > *or full of argument.*
> *I don't want to end up simply having visited this world*
> > > (Oliver, pp. 10-11).

Another poet, Lucille Clifton, conveyed an attitude of hope and courage that I find inspiring and useful not only for my down-days but also as a code for all days.

... she walked away
from the hole in the ground
deciding to live. and she lived (Clifton, p. 20).

Growing up in North Carolina, I heard people like her
described as spunky, determined, or as having feet on
the ground. There
have been days for
me when the choice
has been to live or
to allow the pain or
grief to take over.
And I lived.

There have been days
when the choice has been
to live or to allow the
pain or grief to take over.

Finally, a rhetorical question from Carl Dennis intrigued
me when I first read it. Then with more readings, it
aided me in facing the same question posed by Dennis.

What if the great day never comes
And your life doesn't shine with vivid blossoms,
Just the usual pale variety?
What if the best china never seems called for...

And he goes on to ask, *"Can you will yourself to see a*
common day the way a saint might see it as a gift from
heaven...?" (Dennis, pp. 41-42).

In the midst of grief, it can be terribly challenging to
focus on living. The grief can absorb us and dominate
our lines of vision. To be sure, as you will find on other
pages, it can be crucial to do the grieving. But, I also

believe that we can find ways to allow hope and courage to accompany us. In these four writers, I found a hope that was more

Find ways to allow hope and courage to accompany you.

profound than rose-colored glasses or a naïve cheerful attitude. When my own hope basket was depleted, words like these filled me again. In these words, I found perspectives about living that aided me in my darkest times. I hope they will for you also.

Anger Is A Signal

*A*nger is a signal, and one worth listening to. Our anger may be a message that we are being hurt, that our rights are being violated, that our needs or wants are not being adequately met, or simply that something is not right. Our anger may tell us that we are not addressing an important emotional issue in our lives, or that too much of our self — our beliefs, values, desires, or ambitions — is being compromised in a relationship. Our anger may be a signal that we are doing more and giving more than we can comfortably do or give. Or our anger may warn us that others are doing too much for us, at the expense of our own competence and growth. Just as physical pain tells us to take our hand off the hot stove, the pain of our anger preserves the very integrity of our self (Lerner, p. 1).

Our anger preserves the integrity of the self.

I've included this lengthy quote from Harriet Lerner's book because of the way she challenged its readers to examine their attitudes about anger. Anger, for many people, is the most perplexing of human emotions. We all get angry/feel anger. It is a natural, normal emotion. Like any human emotion, anger is a response to something that is occurring inside or outside of us. Yet, unlike most other emotions, many people question their anger. They begin wondering if they should be angry in the first place. Or they respond to the all-too-common belief that anger is not okay, mature, or wise. Or, "be positive only" rules apply. Self-doubt about the appropriateness of anger is a common response. Lerner described another perspective in the above quote, one I find compelling.

Anger and grief are common companions. How does anger relate to hope? Anger and hope have their own connections - more about their ties just ahead - but they are both frequently tied to grief. When we grieve, it is most often because we lost something ... someone we love, health, a job, our home ... something. In addition to our grieving, many people also experience anger. Anger at the person for dying too soon or driving too fast or under the influence. Anger at God for natural disasters. Anger at the government for not enough advance warning about potential terrorist threats. Anger at ourselves for waiting too long to say or do something. Anger is a signal. So, anger and grief are common companions.

Hope can be dominated or blocked by the anger/

grieving combination OR hope can be grabbed as an act of anger. I remember a woman whose estranged husband had killed her children, the animals, and destroyed their house. She was grieving and she was full of rage at him for what he had done. She also moved quickly to hope. She said to me, "Damn it! He had taken everything from me. He was not going to get me!!" She was not speaking of physical safety. By that time he had been arrested. No, she was speaking of her true self, her soul, her spirit. She realized, even as she was grieving and was in rage at this man, that she could allow that anger to continue to dominate her life, thereby letting him also control her life. And she angrily decided that she would not allow that. She reached for hope instead.

The wounded healer is one who acknowledges the wound and the accompanying grief and anger.

Her story reminds me of the notion of the wounded healer, a long held image in mythology, psychology and theology. The wounded healer is one who acknowledges the wound — be it a personal violation, injury, death ... whatever — and the accompanying grief and anger. But, rather than allow the legitimate anger to grow to fester and become bitterness and hate, the angry and grieving person transforms the anger and becomes a wounded healer. Often people want to help others in their coping. That altruism becomes the motivation for transformation of the anger.

Suffice it to say, not all anger can or should be transformed in this way. Some people volunteer too soon and their ability to help others can be limited because their own grieving deserves primary attention.

An important point about anger. Many people have trouble acknowledging their anger, especially what I have called legitimate anger. The perception is that anger is somehow wrong, dangerous or not the way a "mature" person should respond to a situation. Many people quickly move from anger to a stance of bearing the burden, doing what needs to be done, or assisting others. The result can be what some describe as a sort of passive anger, an anger transformed into resentment and blame. When this occurs, hope can be thwarted.

Have you used your anger to move toward hope?

What is your attitude about anger, including your own? How is your hope related to anger you feel? Have you let your anger, even legitimate anger, get in the way of hope? Or have you used your anger to move toward hope by assertive acts of self-care or altruism?

If this chapter raised more questions than insight, it may be that anger deserves some of your attention. Even that decision can foster hope. Anger can be a reactive emotion. To choose to examine the place of anger in your life moves you back in charge, from reactive to proactive. That is hopeful!

Continuing Bonds

A commonly used metaphor for grieving people is the empty hole. The absence of the deceased person, the breast removed because of cancer, the home burned in a fire or not being able to parent as children grow older ... whatever the loss ... leaves a hole. The pain of that loss is reinforced when the culture wants people to "get over" their losses and quickly return to normal. After the Oklahoma City bombing, there were repeated predictions, as memorial events occurred, that healing and closure would then happen. Even the physical hole left in the bomb's wake had been transformed into a memorial park.

The loss leaves a hole.

Some of the early work of grief professionals added to this impression. Kubler-Ross' stages led predictably from shock and anger to acceptance. Further, many bereavement workers attempted to aid people in "burying the person and moving on". Disengagement from that which was lost was a common goal.

A more recent understanding is captured in the words, continuing bonds (see Klass, Silverman and Nickman). From this perspective survivors maintain continuing bonds with the person or object lost. And it has been further postulated that these continuing bonds can be a healthy part of the survivor's ongoing life.

That, for me, is a very hopeful message!

Long before this current research and writing by grief and bereavement scholars, we can find a poignant and challenging perspective written by theologian Dietrich Bonhoeffer. A bit of background may enrich his words.

Continuing bonds can be a healthy part of the survivor's ongoing life.

Bonhoeffer and others spoke out and tried in many ways to confront the growing threat of Hitler through the Resistance movement. Leaving the safety of the United States, Bonhoeffer returned to his native Germany to continue the struggle with his people. He was arrested in 1943 and ultimately executed at the age of 39 in 1945. In a book of letters and papers from prison, the following can be found in a letter to a friend written on Christmas Eve.

> ...Nothing can fill the gap when we are away from those we love, and it would be wrong to try and find anything.

We must simply hold out and win through. That sounds
very hard at first, but at the same time it is a great
consolation, since leaving the gap unfilled preserves the
bonds between us. It is nonsense to say that God fills the
gap: he does not fill it, but keeps it empty so that our
communion with another may be kept alive, even at the
cost of pain. In the second place the dearer and richer our
memories,

the more
difficult the
separation.

> *We don't gaze all the time*
> *at a valuable present, but get*
> *it out from time to time.*

But grati-
tude converts the pangs of memory into a tranquil joy.
The beauties of the past are not endured as a thorn in the
flesh, but as a gift precious for its own sake. We must not
wallow in our memories or surrender to them, just as we
don't gaze all the time at a valuable present, but get it out
from time to time, and for the rest hide it away as a
treasure we know is there all the time. Treated in this
way, the past can give us lasting joy and inspiration.
Thirdly, times of separation are not a total loss, nor are
they completely unprofitable for our companionship - at
least there is no reason why they should be. In spite of all
the difficulties they bring, they can be wonderful means of
strengthening and deepening fellowship (Bonhoeffer,
pp. 120-121).

For me, the *words…we don't gaze all the time at a valuable*
*present, but get it out from time to time…*are especially
meaningful. Even as I type this, I'm looking on my desk
at a glass paperweight given to me by a dear friend who

died of AIDS in 1993. Each time I pick it up or look at it, I think of my friend and my continuing bond with him. Another friend calls such objects, "worthies," meaning that they are worthy of the memory, worthy of the legacy. The worthy became a reminder of the continuing bond. I didn't want my friend to die. I still miss him. But I want even less to be forced to move on, to disengage. I was the richer because of my connection to my friend. I am the richer still (see Bowman, 1993).

I want even less to be forced to move on.

Can continuing bonds be a useful way of describing your continuing connection with someone or some-thing you have lost? There is a Chinese proverb that goes something like: Each person is like a piece of paper and each passerby leaves a mark. Continuing bonds can be a way of honoring those particular marks and relationships that we choose to continue. Consider your continuing bonds.

Seize or Live In the Moment

*H*ope involves a future story. However, that future story may be the next hour, day, week, even your intention to finish reading this page. Continuing to read these lines is a commitment to the next moment. Throughout the centuries, we have heard messages akin to live fully in the moment. I have been told that for over eight hundred years the Benedictines have practiced a rule that each day is to be treated as the last day of life. From their faith perspective, this does not imply a preoccupation with dying. Rather, one is obliged to live as fully as possible in the moment. A latter day version of this attitude is the commonly expressed rule of hospice care to live as fully as you can for as long as you can.

Live as fully as possible in the moment.

A vivid personal example of practicing a live-in-the-moment attitude can be found in this poem by Irish poet, John Montague.   He wrote of a woman's courage in the face of pain and her determination to seize the moment this way.

> With wife and daughter this evening
> you receive us, smiling, although
>
> paralysed from the waist down, and
> hauled from the electric wheelchair
> to your own table by helpful hands.
>
> Yet splashing out your best wine
> into your guest's glass, or handling
> round the plates, you deride the pain
> your racked body feels, proclaim the joy
> of being allowed some normal time again,
>
> … Leaving,
>
> I will take both your hands in mine,
> although in neither have you any feeling.
>
> Dear specialist in waste, professor of pain,
> with your feebled body, pierced as a pin-cushion,
> you still persist, as if beyond such sickness,
> even beyond death's encroaching ruin,
> there dwelt some final, lasting sweetness
>
> (Montague, p. 65).

Mindfulness is being right where we are.

Mindfulness, according to Buddhist wisdom, is being right where we are. Pema Chodron described mindfulness as being one with our experience, not dissociating, being right there when our hand touches the doorknob or the telephone rings or when feelings of all kinds arise (Chodron, p. 38).

For most of us, that is easier said than done, especially when grieving. But, it can be done with supportive understanding. It may also be aided by the creation of a space — some say a sacred space — that encourages being in the moment. A personal example.

Create space that encourages being in the moment.

A few years ago, my daughter, her husband, and the excited extended family and friends began pointing toward a date on the calendar. You know the one. A due date. The birth of their first child, a grandchild for others, and a playmate for cousins and friends was on the way.

Then, things happened. Complications occurred during the pregnancy. Concern and protective watchfulness became apprehension and anxiety as time passed. Eventually — much more slowly than medically appropriate — a placenta previa was diagnosed. The birth canal was blocked by the placenta meaning that the only delivery method was a caesarian section. There was also a danger of massive bleeding had the natural birth process begun.

Picture a couple who, like many, had planned and worked during the pregnancy for the long-awaited moment. Picture attendance at birth classes and regular check-ins with the medical team. Include minimal reference to anything but a natural delivery by the health care professionals. The husband and father-to-be was ready for his breathing and support assistance. The wife and mother-to-be was ready for the normal, regular birthing experience. Then, placenta previa.

The doctor came to meet with the couple and family. He acknowledged that mistakes had been made. He also caringly clarified what they were facing. Turning to my daughter, he said, *You are bleeding, not hemorrhaging. This will be a special delivery, not an emergency delivery. We do these sorts of special deliveries all the time.* From my perspective, this was a wonderful way of acknowledging what was. He did not minimize realities. Yet, at the same time, the doctor offered important clarity. He also recognized that they were grieving the birth that would not be. The birthing dream they had planned would not occur. The doctor, then, surprised all of us with a gift of space so that the couple particularly could seize their moment. Turning to the two of them, he asked, *When would like your birth?* Power was being given back to people who had just lost power and control. My daughter and her husband turned to each other and quickly gave a time a few hours later. *I'll be available then,* he said. What a marvelous sensitivity to the intersection of grieving and hope! Readiness for an unplanned procedure involved the formation of a new future story. The couple was given time to plan for a caesarian delivery.

Readiness for an unplanned procedure involved the formation of a new future story.

Many people who have lost their future story through a death, loss of job, radical change of health, or personal catastrophe have told me that they now have trouble looking far into the future. They have, as they put it, come to put focus more on the present, on the moment. When the unexpected happens, you know in a more profound way it can happen again.

Ronald Valdiserri wrote about this adjustment in his understanding of hope while a pathologist and researcher at the Centers for Disease Control and Prevention in Atlanta and while his twin brother was battling AIDS. His brother died during the writing of the book from which this is taken.

> *It would be easy to assume that the AIDS epidemic, so often associated with loss, generates nothing but sorrow in those it touches, that the personal adjustments we make are all negative. I find, on the contrary, that AIDS has helped me to clarify just what does and does not matter during our brief time in this world. The epidemic has not taken hope away from me, but it has taught me that inadequacy of looking toward the future as a means of rescue from the present. AIDS has shown me that hope is strongest in us when we seek our fulfillment in the circumstances of the present, when we refuse to defer our dreams or to accept defeat* (Valdiserri, pp. 3-4).

Seize your moments. Make of them something full and rich. *Seize your moments.* Healing is possible even when curing is not. Hope can happen even when things fall apart. Balance your longer hopes with shorter — in the moment — hopes.

Benedictions

Good-byes are hard for most people. Couples struggling with fertility challenges often spend years trying to give birth to a child before ever considering adoption, foster care, or the choice of not having children. Some people won't attend funerals because to do so — to their way of thinking — would be saying good bye. And that would hurt too much. I've been told by people with a spinal chord injury that has left them paralyzed that years later they carry internal pictures of a body still functioning in the old, familiar ways. They can still wake up years after and, if not careful, fall out of bed. It's hard to say good-bye to mobility, to a breast removed, to memory lost through Alzheimer's, to a marriage partner, and to a job ... to name but a few.

It's hard to say good-bye.

Still, we know that loss is a part of life. And grief is a normal part of our everyday lives. In this booklet, we have explored ways to reach for and access hope when dreams have been shattered and we must say good-bye to the dreams, at least in their previous form. That process can be aided by a willingness to engage in benedictions. A benediction is a blessing. A blessing is an affirmation of value and worth; it is a send-off with support; it is a connection to a community. Religious or spiritual groups often use a benediction to mark a transition from worship to service in the community or from a gathering to what follows. It can also be used in healing rituals. Certainly grieving people deserve to be blessed as they strive for equilibrium and meaning.

A benediction is a blessing.

A man was facing major career and life decisions. As a Quaker, Parker Palmer had been taught that insight would come through prayer, his actions, and waiting. He believed that what Quakers call "way" would be found. "Way" did not come as he expected.

> *After a few months of deepening frustration, I took my troubles to an older Quaker woman well known for her thoughtfulness and candor. "Ruth," I said, "people keep telling me that 'way will open.' Well, I sit in the silence, I pray, I listen for my calling, but way is not opening. I've been trying to find my vocation for a long time, and I still don't have the foggiest idea of what I'm meant to do. Way may open for other people, but it's sure not opening for me."*
>
> *Ruth's reply was a model of Quaker plain-speaking. "I'm a birthright Friend," she said somberly, "and in sixty-*

plus years of living, way has never opened in front of me." She paused, and I started sinking into despair. Was this wise woman telling me that the Quaker concept of God's guidance was a hoax?

Then she spoke again, this time with a grin. "But a lot of way has closed behind me, and that's had the same guiding effect."

Palmer then acknowledged that there was as much guidance in what did not and cannot happen in life as there was in what can and does — maybe more (Palmer, pp. 38-39). Blessings come in strange and mysterious ways.

Norman Cousins didn't use the word benediction, but he did suggest, in this passage, the importance of blessing each living moment. In the text there is the implication that if life is lived well, dying and death will be easier. Good-byes might lose some of the sting.

Hope, faith, love and a strong will to live offer no promise of immortality, only proof of our uniqueness as human beings and opportunity to experience full growth even under the grimmest circumstances. The clock provides only a technical measurement of how long we live. Far more real than the ticking of time is the way we open up the minutes and invest them with meaning. Death is not the ultimate tragedy in life. The ultimate tragedy is to die without discovering the possibilities of full growth. The approach of death need not be denial of that growth (Cousins, p. 25).

Inspiring words, yes, AND hard words to live out. It's not easy to grant or receive benedictions when the endings being experienced are ones we wish were not happening in the first place. Still, what choice do we have? If indeed the unwanted change is occurring - the divorce is about to be granted, lupus has been diagnosed, layoffs have been announced, the funeral is tomorrow - we can either remain bitter about the loss or

We can either remain bitter or attempt to be a blessing.

attempt to grant ourselves and others a blessing, even while we still grieve.

A benedictory blessing is neither rose-colored glasses nor avoidance of reality. Rather, seeking or accepting a benediction is an effort to find grounding, solace, meaning, or, in other words, a blessing for the harsh reality. Hospices around the world strive to aid the dying in living as fully as they can for as long as they can. A benediction!

Jane Kenyon wrote her own benediction. But because it is also so human and compelling it has become a benediction for many. Drawing on metaphors surrounding the farm on which she lived, she gave us these words:

> *Let the light of late afternoon*
> *shine through chinks in the barn, moving*
> *up the bales as the sun moves down.*

Let the cricket take up chafing
as a woman takes up her needles
and her yarn. Let evening come.

... To the bottle in the ditch, to the scoop
in the oats, to air in the lung
let evening come.

Let it come, as it will, and don't
be afraid. God does not leave us
comfortless, so let evening come (Kenyon, p. 69).

Good-byes aren't easy. They are hard for most people. One may say, "I didn't want this. I don't want this. But, damn it, I'm going to do the best I can with what I've got." Another might say, "This would not have been my way. I don't like the way this turned out. I wish there was another way. But, this is the way and I'm determined to see my way through it with my pride and dignity in place."

Let evening come.

Let evening come. And may your benediction contain a blessing for the evenings and mornings ahead.

A Page for Your Reflections

Hope is not optimism. Optimism tends to minimize the tragic sense of life or foster the belief that the remedy to life's ills is simple. The hoping person is fully aware of the harshness and losses of life .... Hope is the sense of possibility; in despair and in trouble, it is the sense of a way out and a destiny that goes somewhere, even if not to the specific place one had in mind (Fairchild, pp. 50-51).

An Afterword

*I*n the beginning of this booklet, I suggested that hope is personal. Hope, I wrote, does not easily conform to a framework or an orderly step-by-step process. I also suggested that one of the best ways of accessing hope was through stories of hope. The preceding pages of stories then followed. As I read and re-read the many accounts of hope, I looked for themes. Here are five that I found repeatedly in the personal and literary stories found in the booklet. I share them now for your consideration.

- *Hope includes a future story.*
- *Hope includes a shared story.*
- *Hope includes stories of meaning.*
- *Hope includes an affirmative story.*
- *Hope includes the real story.*

Resources Cited in the Booklet

Becker, Gay (1997) *Disrupted lives: how people create meaning in a chaotic world* Berkeley: University of California Press, p. 4.

Berry, Wendell (1985) *Collected poems 1957-1982* San Francisco: North Point Press., p. 69.

Bonhoeffer, Dietrich (1953) *Letters and papers from prison.* New York: Macmillan Paperbacks, pp. 120-121.

Boss, Pauline (1999) *Ambiguous Loss.* Cambridge: Harvard University Press.

Bowman, Ted (1993) "Gift Leaves Reflection of a Valued Friend" *Star-Tribune*, March 15, 1993.

Bowman, Ted (1994) *Loss of dreams: a special kind of grief* . St. Paul: chapbook.

Bowman, Ted (1998) "Too Many Platitudes," unpublished poem.

Bowman, Ted (2001) "Distinctions," unpublished poem.

Broyard, Anatole (1992) *Intoxicated by my illness.* New York: Clarkson Potter Publishers, p. 43.

Chodron, Pema (1997) *When things fall apart: heart advice for difficult times.* Boston: Shambhala, p. 38.

Clifton, Lucille (1993) "she lived" from *The book of light.* Port Townsend, WA: Copper Canyon Press, p. 20.

Cording, Robert (1999) "Fireflies," from *Image: The Journal of the Arts and Religion*, No. 22, Winter/Spring, pp. 27-28.

Couglin, Ruth (1993) *Grieving: a love story.* New York: HarperPerennial. pp. 34-35.

Cousins, Norman (1989) *Head first: the biology of hope*. New York: E.P. Dutton, pp. 25 and 66.

Dass, Ram and Gorman, Paul (1985) *How can I help?* New York: Alfred A. Knopf, p. 27.

Dennis, Carl (1997) "The Great Day" from *Ranking the wishes*. New York: Penguin Books, pp. 41-42.

Fairchild, Roy W. (1980) *Finding Hope again: a pastor's guide to counseling depressed persons*. San Francisco: Harper & Row, Publishers, pp. 50-51.

Frank, Arthur W. (1991) *At the will of the body: reflections on illness*. Boston: Houghton Mifflin Company, p. 38 and p. 40.

Frank, Arthur W. (1995.). *The wounded storyteller: body, illness, and ethics*. Chicago: The University of Chicago Press, p. xii.

Gill, Barbara (1997) *Changed by a child: companion notes for parents of a child with a disability*. New York: Doubleday, p.16.

Hikmet, Nazim (1994) "On Living," from *Poems of Nazim Hikmet*, translated by Randy Blasing and Mutlu Konuk. New York: Persea Books, pp. 128-130.

Hughes, Langston (1994) "The Dream Keeper," from *The dream keeper and other poems*. New York: Alfred A. Knopf, p. 2

Jamison, Kay Redfield (1995) *An unquiet mind: a memoir of mood and madness*. New York: Alfred A. Knopf, p. 118.

Kenyon, Jane (1990) "Let Evening Come" from *Let evening come: poems*. St. Paul: Graywolf Press, p. 69

Kingsolver, Barbara (1995) *High tide in Tucson*. New York: HarperCollins Publishers, pp. 15-16.

Klass, Dennis, Silverman, Phyllis, R. and Nickman, Steven L. (eds) (1996) *Continuing bonds: new understandings of grief*. Bristol, PA: Taylor & Francis.

Lamott, Anne (1999) *Traveling mercies: some thoughts on faith*. New York: Pantheon Books, pp. 68-73

Lerner, Harriet Goldhor (1985) *The dance of anger*. New York: HarperCollins, p. 1.

Lester, Andrew C. (1995) *Hope in pastoral care and counseling*. Louisville: Westminster John Knox Press, pp. 29-30.

Lorde, Audre (1980) *The cancer journals*. San Francisco: Spinsters/Aunt Lute, p. 76.

Mairs, Nancy (1990) *Carnal acts: essays*. New York: HarperPerennial, pp. 114-115.

Mairs, Nancy (1997)."Letting Go," *Christian Century*. November 5, 1997, p. 1014.

Meyers, Kent (1998) *The witness of combines*. Minneapolis: The University of Minnesota Press, p. 20.

Middlebrook, Christina (1996) *Seeing the crab: a memoir of dying*. New York: Basic Books, p. 31.

Mitchell, Kenneth R. and Anderson, Herbert (1983) *All our losses/all our griefs* Louisville: The Westminster/John Knox Press.

Montague, John (1999) "Remission" from *Smashing the piano*. Loughcrew, Oldcastle, County Meath, Ireland: The Gallery Press, p. 65.

Oliver, Mary (1992) "When Death Comes," from *New and selected poems*. Boston: Beacon Press, pp. 10-11.

Osborn, Claudia L. (1998) *Over my head: a doctor's own story of head injury from the inside looking out*. Kansas City: Andrews McMeel Publishing, pp. 116-119.

Palmer, Parker (2000) *Let your life speak: listening for the voice of vocation*. San Francisco: Jossey-Bass Publisher, pp. 38-39.

Pringle, Terry (1992) *This is the child: a father's story of his young son's battle with leukemia*. Dallas: Southern Methodist University Press, p. 186.

Remen, Rachel (1996) *Kitchen table wisdom: stories that heal*. New York: Riverhead Books, pp. 151-152.

Sheepshanks, Mary (1997) *The bird of my loving: a personal response to loss and grief*. London: Michael Joseph LTD, pp. 2-3 and pp. 140-141.

Silverstein, Shel (1987) "The Little Boy And The Old Man" From *Free to be... a family* by Marlo Thomas and Friends. New York: Bantam Books, p. 105.

Spiegel, David (1993) *Living beyond limits: new hope and help in facing life-threatening illness*. New York: Times Books, p. 104.

Tamaro, Susanna (1998) *Follow your heart*. London: Vintage, pp. 55-56.

Valdiserri, Ronald O. (1994) *Gardening in clay: reflections on AIDS*. Ithaca: Cornell University Press, pp. 3-4.

Veninga, Robert (1985) *A gift of hope: how we survive our tragedies*. Boston: Little, Brown & Company.

West, Cornel (1993) *Race matters*. Boston: Beacon Press, p. 15.

*T*his booklet, like my life, reflects the influence of many persons and situations. Hopeful people have taught me much of what I know about the subject. For their witness and example I am grateful.

This booklet is dedicated to my parents Ralph and Bertie Bowman for their years of living hope. Thank you!

Dedicated to my parents for their years of living hope.

Special thanks to colleagues who offered their comments about drafts of this booklet as it evolved over the months. A sign of friendship is honest reaction to someone's ideas and manner of expression. I received many signs. The booklet is better because of their input.

Two women deserve more than mention. Marge Grahn-Bowman, my wife, and Nancy Parker Hokonson, my friend and the person who moved my words into this format, have exhibited patience, perseverance, creativity, keen editorial skills, and the best forms of support from the beginning of this project to its publication. There is no way I can thank them enough for their commitment to the publication of these pages.

Additional booklets can be ordered for $8.50 (US $) each from the address listed below. This amount includes the postage and handling costs for mailings within the United States. Costs for mailing to other countries must be added. Special rates are available for 30 or more copies sent to any location.

Ted Bowman travels throughout the United States and abroad leading workshops, consulting, and speaking about grief and loss, shattered dreams, hope, resiliency, and the impact these have for persons, families, helpers, organizations, and communities. Contact him if interested at:

Ted Bowman
2111 Knapp Street
St. Paul, MN 55108-1814
USA

Phone: 651/645-6058
Fax: 651/645-6326
Email: bowma008@tc.umn.edu